OCT   2014

SEA HORSES

SAMANTHA BELL

Published in the United States of America by Cherry Lake Publishing
Ann Arbor, Michigan
www.cherrylakepublishing.com

Consultants: Dominique A. Didier, PhD, Associate Professor, Department of Biology, Millersville University;
Marla Conn, ReadAbility, Inc.
Book design and illustration: Sleeping Bear Press

Photo Credits: ©Joe Belanger/Shutterstock Images, cover, 1, 8; ©Arnon Polin/Shutterstock Images, 5; ©midnight_sun/
iStockphoto, 7; ©Benjamin Pardini/Dreamstime.com, 11; ©Dorling Kindersley RF/Thinkstock, 13; ©semet/
iStockphoto, 15; ©Jonpaul Hosking/Shutterstock Images, 17; ©Dan Exton/Shutterstock Images, 19; ©skynesher/
iStockphoto, 21; ©Elizabeth Haslam/ http://www.flickr.com/ CC-BY-2.0, 22; ©Piotr Rzeszutek/Shutterstock Images, 25;
©Stephane Bidouze/Shutterstock Images, 26; ©Andrea Izzotti/Shutterstock Images, 29

Library of Congress Cataloging-in-Publication Data

Bell, Samantha, author.
Sea horses / Samantha Bell.
    pages cm. — (Exploring our oceans)
  Summary: "Introduces facts about sea horses, including physical features, habitat, life cycle, food,
and threats to these ocean creatures. Photos, captions, and keywords supplement the narrative of
this informational text"— Provided by publisher.
  Audience: 8-12.
  Audience: Grades 4 to 6.
  Includes bibliographical references and index.
  ISBN 978-1-62431-604-3 (hardcover) — ISBN 978-1-62431-616-6 (pbk) —
ISBN 978-1-62431-628-9 (pdf) — ISBN 978-1-62431-640-1 (ebook)
  1. Sea horses—Juvenile literature. I. Title.

  QL638.S9B45 2014
  597.6798—dc23   2013040968

Cherry Lake Publishing would like to acknowledge the work of
The Partnership for 21st Century Skills. Please visit www.p21.org
for more information.

Printed in the United States of America
Corporate Graphics Inc.
January 2014

ABOUT THE AUTHOR

Samantha Bell is a children's writer and illustrator living in South Carolina with her husband, four
children, and lots of animals. She has illustrated a number of picture books, including some of her
own. She has also written magazine articles, stories, and poems, as well as craft, activity, and wildlife
books. She loves animals, being outdoors, and learning about all the amazing wonders of nature.

TABLE OF CONTENTS

CHAPTER 1

A SMALL SEA LEGEND

They've been a part of stories and legends for hundreds of years. Herds of them can be found in meadows of sea grass. Their heads look a lot like those of horses. But you can't ride these animals. With monkey-like tails, lizard-like eyes, and a kangaroo-type pouch, sea horses are some of the ocean's most unusual creatures.

Despite their strange appearance, sea horses are actually fish. They have gills to breathe underwater. They have fins to push themselves up and down and forward and backward.

Sea horses can blend into their surroundings.

There are somewhere between 34 and 50 species of sea horses. No one knows the exact number because sea horses are difficult to identify. They can change their colors and patterns to match their surroundings, so members of the same **species** don't always look alike. Often, one species of sea horse will be given several different names. To accurately identify a sea horse, scientists must count the number of bony rays in their fins and the bony rings that encircle their body and tail. Scientists also compare the length of the sea horses' snouts and head spines.

Sea horses can be found in mild and tropical waters throughout the world. They swim in every sea and ocean except for the coldest ones near the poles. Some species live as far north as Canada, the United Kingdom, and northern Norway. Others live as far south as southern New Zealand and Argentina.

Sea horses make their homes on the **continental shelves** near the coasts. In some places on these shelves, coral and sponges can attach to form reefs. Algae, sea grass, and seaweed grow on the reefs. Sea horses anchor themselves here, sometimes to just a single blade of sea grass.

These amazing animals adapt their behavior to attach to man-made items, too. They've been found living around **jetties** and piers, as well as ropes and old machinery. If there is something to hold on to and food to eat, sea horses will settle there.

Because they can't swim against the ocean currents, sea horses tend to stay near their homes. Males might

A sea horse uses its tail to hold on to plants that live in the water.

As more of the ocean is explored, scientists will continue to learn about sea horses.

travel as little as 3 feet (1 m) their whole lives. Females will go about 30 feet (9 m) in search of food. Some sea horses move between shallow and deep water, depending on the season. The ones that move farther out find a floating shelter, such as sargassum, a type of brown floating seaweed.

Sea horses can also be found in the slightly salty waters of **estuaries** and **mangrove swamps**. These areas provide a good place for sea horses to give birth because they don't have many waves or currents. There are dangers, however. The rainy season sometimes brings too much freshwater. This affects water quality and can harm sea horses. Also, estuaries are tidal. When the tide goes out, the sea horses can become trapped. In the mangrove swamps, thick mud can build up.

Although scientists have learned a lot about sea horses, there is much more to discover. Sea horses can be difficult to find. Most of the ocean has not been explored, and there are probably unknown species. Sea horses remain a mystery of the seas.

THINK ABOUT IT

READ THIS CHAPTER CLOSELY. WHICH FACTS ABOUT SEA HORSES SURPRISED YOU THE MOST? WHICH FACTS DID YOU ALREADY KNOW?

Sea Horses Are Fish

From the tip of their stretched-out tails to the top of their heads, sea horses range in size from less than 1 inch (2.5 cm) to more than 1 foot (30.5 cm) long. The largest is the Australian big belly or potbelly sea horse, measuring 12 to 14 inches (30.5 to 35.5 cm). The smallest sea horse is the pygmy sea horse. It measures from .5 to .66 inches (1.3 to 1.7 cm). That's about as long as your thumbnail!

Ancient Greeks and Romans used to imagine the sea horses rising up on the foam of the waves. But sea horses aren't strong swimmers at all. Unlike other fish, they

This potbelly sea horse gets its name from its large belly.

don't have a caudal fin, or tail fin, to push themselves through the water. Instead, a sea horse moves slowly forward using the dorsal fin on its back, fluttering it about 20 to 35 times each second. Two small pectoral fins, located behind and on each side of the fish's head, help as well. The sea horse also uses the pectoral fins to steer and change directions.

As sea horses move through the water, they keep their bodies upright. They have a swim bladder, a sac that is full of gas to help them float. By changing the volume of the gas in their bladder, they can move up and down in the water like a submarine.

Because sea horses are poor swimmers, they attach themselves to other objects. Sea horses use their **prehensile** tails to anchor themselves. They will grab hold of anything, even your hand! They may latch onto a piece of coral or sea grass, but man-made objects will do just as well. Sometimes they attach themselves to sargassum, traveling long distances as it floats with the currents. Even while swimming in a group, sea horses will constantly try to grasp each other's tails or snouts. If the ends of the tails are ever damaged or broken, they'll grow back again.

Sea horses are unlike other fish in another way. They don't have any scales. Instead, they have thin layers of bony plates that are covered with thin skin. The plates

BODY DIAGRAM

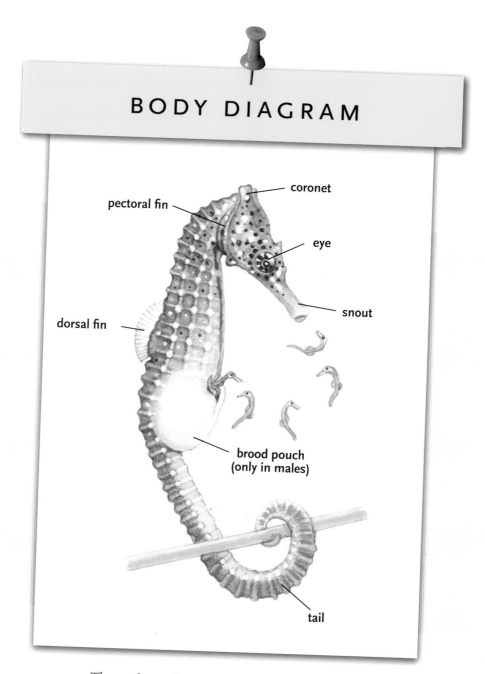

coronet

pectoral fin

eye

snout

dorsal fin

brood pouch
(only in males)

tail

The male sea horse gives birth to the babies.

look like rings around the sea horse. There are usually about 12 rings around its body and 33 to 48 rings around its tail.

At the top of a sea horse's head is the **coronet**. It comes in a variety of sizes, angles, knobs, and spikes. The coronet of a sea horse is like a human fingerprint. Every sea horse has a different coronet. Not only can different species be identified by the coronet, but each individual sea horse can, too.

Because of the bony plates, sea horses cannot bend. They also cannot turn their heads from side to side. But they can still see everything going on around them. That's because sea horses can move their eyes independently of each other. This allows them to look forward and backward at the same time.

This sea horse is barely visible among the green sea plants.

LOOK AGAIN

LOOK AT THE SEA HORSE'S PREHENSILE TAIL IN THIS PHOTOGRAPH. CAN YOU THINK OF ANY OTHER ANIMALS THAT HAVE A PREHENSILE TAIL?

AMBUSHING DINNER

Sea horses are predators and eat smaller animals. But they don't chase their prey. Instead, they ambush it.

Sea horses have an amazing ability to **camouflage** themselves. They can change the color and texture of their skin to look like their surroundings. Sea horses are white, gray, pink, green, orange, yellow, red, black, or brown. They can have spots, lines, or splotches. But in an instant, they can completely change these colors and patterns.

A sea horse in disguise might look like speckled

The texture of this sea horse matches the texture of the plants.

gravel, a strand of sea grass, or a bright piece of coral. Some species of sea horses can even lengthen their spines. Others spend a few days growing extra **appendages** that look like seaweed. Later, if they don't need the appendages anymore, they'll lose them. Mossy sea horses grow a coat to match the weedy area where they live. All of these camouflaged sea horses will stay almost motionless until their prey swims close enough. Then, with a quick snap of each sea horse's head, the prey is eaten.

Sea horses feed on many small organisms, even **microscopic** ones. Fish and crab larvae, plankton, worms, and other small **invertebrates** are among the favorites. Sea horses don't have any teeth, so they can't chew their food. Instead, they have long, bony snouts. They use their snouts like a straw, sucking up the prey whole. Sometimes the organism is too big to fit in the sea horse's snout. When this happens, the sea horse smashes it in half with its jaws. Then it eats it.

Sea horses don't have stomachs either. Because of this, they digest their food very quickly. This leaves them with a huge appetite, and they must eat almost all the time to stay alive. Sea horses will swallow from 50 to 300 organisms an hour. They use their unusual eyes to keep a constant lookout for the next meal.

Though sea horses don't whinny, they do make noise. Some have been known to make a clicking sound as they feed. When heard underwater, the noise sounds like someone smacking his or her lips. Scientists believe sea horses make these sounds by scraping one bone against another bone, the same way a cricket rubs its legs together. Sea horses also make these sounds as they search for a mate.

Camouflage is a way for sea horses to hide from predators.

LOOK AGAIN

THE SEA HORSE IN THIS PHOTOGRAPH IS CAMOUFLAGED FOR PROTECTION. CAN YOU THINK OF ANY OTHER ANIMALS THAT USE CAMOUFLAGE?

A COURTSHIP DANCE

Because sea horses aren't good swimmers, searching for a mate can be risky. So when a sea horse finds a mate, the two often stay together for the whole breeding season. This gives the pair of sea horses more time to have offspring.

Attracting a female sea horse isn't easy. It starts with a long courtship dance that can last from a few hours to several days. The male begins by bowing his head. Then he performs a complicated dance around the female. Sometimes he wraps his tail around her. Other times he

[21ST CENTURY SKILLS LIBRARY]

The male sea horse will sometimes hold the tail of a female sea horse.

copies her movements. He might also change colors.
If the female accepts him, she joins in the dance.
They link their tails together and move through the
sea grass in an underwater ballet.

Even after they've found a mate, sea horses continue to dance. They greet each other every morning with a dance that's all their own. The dance helps strengthen their bond. It also shows them that their partner is alive and well. Then they separate for the rest of the day.

Like many fish, a female sea horse lays eggs. But that's where the similarities end. When sea horses mate, it's the male who becomes pregnant!

Eggs grow in the pouch of the male sea horse.

The male sea horse has a pouch in the front, much like a kangaroo. Depending on the species, the female will lay up to 1,500 eggs in the pouch. The eggs are **fertilized** by the male. As the young develop, they receive extra oxygen and other nutrients. Then the fluid in the pouch begins to change. It becomes more like seawater. This will make it easier for the newborn sea horses to move from the pouch into the ocean.

Incubation time varies with each species. Sometime between 10 days and 6 weeks, the eggs hatch. In what seems like an explosion of babies, the male gives birth by pushing them out of the pouch. These tiny fry, or newly hatched fish, look just like their parents. Within a few hours, the male is ready for more eggs.

The hundreds of newborn sea horses are on their own. They will drift away with the ocean currents until they settle in a new place. Only about five or six of every 200 to 300 will become adults. But those that do survive can live up to four years.

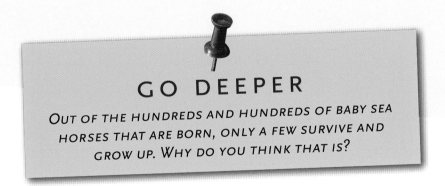

GO DEEPER

OUT OF THE HUNDREDS AND HUNDREDS OF BABY SEA HORSES THAT ARE BORN, ONLY A FEW SURVIVE AND GROW UP. WHY DO YOU THINK THAT IS?

Threats from Weather

Adult sea horses don't have many natural enemies. Their stiff, bony armor keeps most predators away. Animals that do eat them must eat them whole. Fish such as tuna, cod, snappers, and sharks will eat a sea horse. Rays, crabs, sea turtles, and fairy penguins also add them to their menu.

Baby sea horses are in much greater danger. Some species begin life near the surface of the water. They have nowhere to hide and nothing to hang on to. They are often eaten by fish and seabirds. Others grow up near the ocean floor. They might be eaten by sea anemones or crustaceans.

The biggest natural threat to sea horses comes from storms. Strong waves can pull the sea horses from their grass or coral supports. In such rough waters, the sea horses must work hard to swim. They often die of exhaustion or are washed ashore.

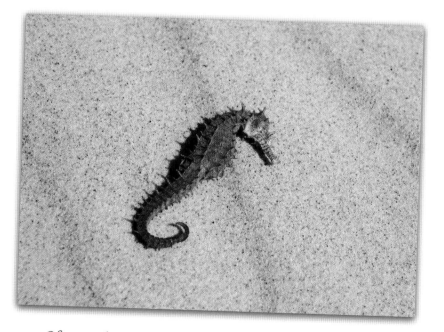

Often sea horses are not strong enough to survive storms.

In some cultures sea horses have been used as medicine for hundreds of years.

But there are other dangers to sea horses. Sadly, they come from people. As many as 24 million sea horses are caught and sold each year. Most of them are used in traditional Chinese medicine. In some cultures, it is believed that sea horses can cure a number of health problems, including asthma, heart disease, and broken bones.

Sea horses are also taken for other reasons. Dried sea horses are sold as souvenirs. They are used in jewelry, key chains, and other crafts. Live sea horses are sold to aquarium owners. However, they are difficult to keep because they have special water and food requirements. Many of them die in captivity. Even more sea horses are accidentally caught by shrimp fishers.

Sea horse **habitats** are in danger, too. The coral reefs, sea grass beds, mangrove swamps, and coastal areas that sea horses make their home have also become our favorite places. Human activity and development are slowly destroying them. Coral reefs that grow only about 1 inch (2.5 cm) each year can be damaged in an instant by a tourist. Pollution increases the danger, because much of the waste from cities ends up in the ocean.

Sea horses were once much more abundant. Today the number of sea horses in the wild continues to decrease. The International Union for Conservation of Nature classifies one species as **Endangered**. This means that populations have a very high risk of becoming **extinct**.

But there are things we can do. Governments can monitor their international trade of wild sea horses. Tourists can refuse to buy dried sea horses in craft shops and beach stores. Fish farmers can raise sea horses for public and private aquariums. We can take care of our own local waters and protect them from pollution. This helps keep sea horse habitats safe, even if they are miles away.

The biggest obstacle we face in protecting the sea horses is that we don't know much about them. We don't know exactly how many species there are. We don't know where they all live. We don't know just how they are affected by problems in their habitats. But if we are to help the sea horses, we need to find the answers. And in doing so, we will better understand one of the ocean's most amazing creatures.

There are ways people can help protect sea horses from becoming extinct.

LOOK AGAIN

Look closely at this photograph. What does it tell you about where sea horses live?

THINK ABOUT IT

- When the ancient Greeks and Romans found sea horses washed up on the beach, they created stories about them. They told of fierce sea horses that pulled the chariots of Poseidon (the Greek god of the sea) and Neptune (the Roman god of the sea) through the water. If you had found a sea horse on the beach and didn't know what it was, how might you have explained it?

- In chapter 4, you learned about a sea horse courtship dance. Do you know of other creatures that use a courtship dance for mating?

- Sometimes sea horse is spelled as one word, and sometimes it is spelled as two words. Look in other sources to determine why there are two ways to spell sea horse.

LEARN MORE

FURTHER READING

James, Sylvia M. *Seahorses*. New York: Mondo Publishing, 2002.

Miller, Susan Swan. *Seahorses, Pipefishes, and Their Kin*. New York: Scholastic, 2003.

Turner, Pamela S. *Project Seahorse*. Boston: Houghton Mifflin, 2010.

WEB SITES

Animal Planet—Ultimate Animal Dads
http://animal.discovery.com/tv-shows/animal-planet-presents/videos
/ultimate-animal-dads-sea-horse-dads.htm
Go to this Web site to watch a video on sea horse dads.

National Geographic Kids—Seahorses
http://kids.nationalgeographic.com/kids/animals/creaturefeature/seahorses
Look at photos, read fun facts, and see a map of where sea horses live.

National Wildlife Federation—Seahorses
https://www.nwf.org/Kids/Ranger-Rick/Animals/Fish/Seahorses.aspx
Learn more about several species of sea horses.

GLOSSARY

appendages (uh-PEN-dih-jiz) parts of an organism that stick out

camouflage (KAM-uh-flahj) an animal's natural coloring that enables it to blend in with its surroundings

continental shelves (kahn-tuh-NEN-tuhl SHELVZ) the areas of the seafloor near a coastline

coronet (kawr-uh-NET) the bony plates on the top of the sea horse's head that resemble a crown

endangered (en-DAYN-jurd) at risk of becoming extinct or of dying out

estuaries (ES-choo-er-eez) mouths of rivers where the tide meets the stream

extinct (ik-STINGKT) no longer found alive

fertilized (FUR-tuh-lyzd) the union of an egg with sperm

habitats (HAB-ih-tats) the places where animals or plants naturally live

incubation (in-kyuh-BEY-shuhn) the process of keeping eggs at a certain temperature so that they will develop

invertebrates (in-VUR-tuh-brits) animals without a backbone

jetties (JET-eez) barriers built to protect a harbor or coast

mangrove swamps (MAN-grohv SWOMPS) coastal wetlands in tropical climates characterized by salt-loving trees and plants

microscopic (mye-kruh-SKAH-pik) so small it can only be seen with a microscope

prehensile (pree-HEN-suhl) able to grasp

species (SPEE-sheez) one type, or kind of plant or animal

INDEX